THE BOOK OF
TEA & COFFEE

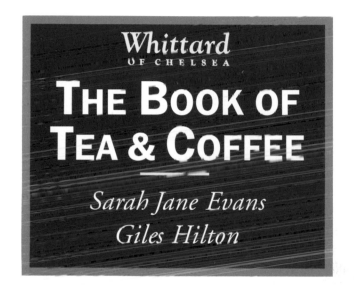

Whittard
OF CHELSEA

THE BOOK OF
TEA & COFFEE

Sarah Jane Evans

Giles Hilton

PAVILION

First published in Great Britain in 1998 by
PAVILION BOOKS LIMITED
London House, Great Eastern Wharf, Parkgate Road, London SW11 4NQ

Text © Sarah Jane Evans and Giles Hilton 1998
Design and layout © Pavilion Books Ltd. 1998

The moral right of the authors has been asserted

Designed by Andrew Barron & Collis Clements Associates
Illustrations by Janice Nicolson

A CIP catalogue record for this book is available from the British Library.

ISBN 1 86205 201 8

Set in Adobe Garamond and ITC Franklin Gothic

Printed in Italy by Jonson Editorial

2 4 6 8 10 9 7 5 3 1

This book can be ordered direct from the publisher. Please contact the
Marketing Department. But try your bookshop first.
Also available from Whittard of Chelsea
Customer Service Freephone Number: 0800 525 092

CONTENTS

TEA

The first cup moistens my lips and throat;
The second cup breaks my loneliness;
The third cup searches my barren entrail but to find therein some
five thousand volumes of odd ideographs;
The fourth cup raises a slight perspiration – all the wrongs of life
pass out through my pores;
At the fifth cup I am purified;
The sixth cup calls me to the realms of the immortals.
The seventh cup – ah, but I could take no more! I only feel the
breath of the cool wind that raises in my sleeves.
Where is Elysium? Let me ride on this sweet breeze and
waft away thither.

Lu T'ung, T'ang Dynasty (AD 620–907)

THE SILVER TEAPOT used to take pride of place on so many Sunday tea-tables. It shone amid the sparkling jellies, the thinly cut sandwiches, the Cheddar cheese and York ham, the homemade jams and the rich fruit cake. What's remarkable about this weekly ritual called 'Tea' was that the children who ate up all the food were prevented from enjoying the centrepiece, the amber liquid which gave the meal its name. Children Didn't (and still don't) Drink Tea.

> *Tea, although an Oriental,*
> *Is a gentleman at least;*
> *Cocoa is a cad and coward,*
> *Cocoa is a vulgar beast.*
>
> G.K. Chesterton,
> *The Song of Right and Wrong*

Princess Victoria, as a child 170 years ago, was denied the reviving cuppa. Her governess disapproved of it. So, the story goes, one of the first things the young Queen did after her coronation in 1838 was to exercise her newly won authority by ordering a cup of tea.

At some point most young people acquire the habit and thereafter it's central to life's rites of passage, with a tea to suit every mood. It can be an elegant drink, delicately perfumed, accompanying the finest of pastries. Or it can be a rich, refreshing brew, ideal for reviving the late afternoon.

For a cup of tea to remember, take the Night Mail to Darjeeling from Calcutta. The journey towards the Himalayas where some of the world's best teas are grown is slow and frustrating for a visitor keen to reach the distant home of some of the world's greatest teas. By morning the traveller is exhausted by a mixture of weariness and excited anticipation. But there's a time-honoured reviver: Indian Railways Masala tea, which should be prescribed at stations and airports the world over. This aromatic and spicy tea is sweet with sugar and thick with milk. A long way from the finesse of Darjeeling's finest, but a perfect restorative.

In the tea gardens of Darjeeling in the foothills of the Himalayas tea is drunk freshly picked and processed, and brewed in pure spring water from the highest mountains. It's impossible to re-create that experience in polluted cities halfway across the world. But today we can go a long way towards it. There's a greater demand than ever for speciality teas, for teas grown, processed and packed to the highest standards.

Tea is relatively simple to brew at home and the great attraction in every culture is the ritual surrounding it. Tea is the drink of friendship, offered before anything else when guests arrive. Tea demands time. Enjoying a cup of tea implies a break, however short, from the usual routine. That's why until recently it was rarely drunk at business breakfasts or power lunches or dinners. Coffee is the digestif, the stimulant for the next round of labour. Coffee, frankly, is the drink with attitude. Tea is altogether cosier and more comforting. No wonder that it's the world's most popular drink, after water.

As tea drinkers know, the world is divided into two halves not by politics – East and West – but by tea consumption – green tea or black tea. The following pages celebrate the many different varieties within these two broad groups, from the black teas of India to the green teas and oolongs of China and Japan, and the pleasures of a fresh, bright cup of tea.

THE TEA LEAF comes from the *Camellia sinensis* bush, a distant relative of the showy, shiny-leaved camellia that brings glamour to gardens in the early spring. It's just the very tip of each branch that goes to make the perfect cup, and the best teas are still picked by hand far away across the world.

Where did it all begin? The story goes that a leaf fell into the water being boiled for the Emperor Shen Nung in 2737 BC and he instantly recognized its medicinal qualities. Later it was described as the elixir of immortality. By AD 450 tea was a recognized medicine, and just over a century later the Buddhist monks were introducing it to Japan. In 780 during the T'ang Dynasty, the poet Lu Yu wrote the great *Ch'a Ching*, the *Book of Tea*. At this time the custom grew of donating the best tea of the spring harvest to the Emperor. Tea leaves in those days could be crumbled and pressed into bricks, which meant they could be transported easily. The tea could then be broken off as required (it is still possible to find these bricks occasionally on sale). By the end of the first millennium the powdered tea was being whipped in a bowl, creating a frothy green drink very similar to that still made in the Japanese tea ceremony.

Tea caught on quickly in the West, though it's interesting to note that what was being drunk was delicately perfumed green tea, not the rich, full-bodied black teas that are usual today. In the early days, says J.G. Houssaye in his *Monographie du Thé*, 'the way to prepare tea was scarcely known in England except in several houses in the capital. The widow of the unfortunate Duke of Monmouth sent a pound of tea to one of her relatives in Scotland, without indicating how it was to be prepared, and

the cook boiled the plant, tossed out the water and served the leaves like a dish of spinach.'

The first tea auction in London was held in Mincing Lane in 1657. In France, Italy and Spain tea was a drink for the upper classes with all the delicate paraphernalia of china and ritual to match. In England and the Netherlands, though, it was enjoyed by all classes. In those days 'tea' was pronounced to rhyme with 'tay', as in this extract from Alexander Pope's *Rape of the Lock*, about Queen Anne:

Here thou, great Anna, whom three realms obey,
Dost sometimes counsel take, and sometimes tea.

This was written in 1711, but from other writers it looks as if usage changed soon after to 'tee'.

*Ecstasy is a glass full of
tea and a piece of sugar
in the mouth.*
Alexander Pushkin

Initially it was an expensive item – hence the culture of the tea caddy locked by the mistress of the house. Smuggling tea was big business in England in those early days to avoid Cromwell's tax.

The taxation of tea was among the events that led to the American War of Independence. The English colonies were not going to pay tax on tea – or on glass; they'd enjoy other drinks, and drink out of tin or china. Since they had no members in London's House of Commons, they could rightly object to taxation without representation. The arrival of ships laden with tea, priced high enough to ensure the East India Company retained its profit, was the trigger. The tea was dumped in Boston harbour, and the colonies were ready to rise up. This was the first real blow to the East India Company, which had run a very profitable trade under its impressive monopoly. The Company traded opium for tea, enslaving generations of Chinese to the drug.

The British were very keen to break the Chinese hold on tea supply and had been attempting to grow plants in India. Though jungle needed to be cleared the climate was good. The only problem was they did not know how to process the leaves. East India Company traders stayed in their *hongs* (warehouses) in Canton and on the 'English Island', Hong Kong, and were not permitted to travel further afield. Robert Fortune made the difference. Dressed as a Chinese merchant he travelled through the forbidden tea regions in the 1820s, making careful observations. He returned with seeds for planting in India and the ability to process the leaves. Around the same time *Camellia sinensis* was found growing wild in Assam, which saved the day for the English planters.

The first of the Empire teas was sold in Mincing Lane in London in 1839. These Indian teas were characteristically bolder and blacker than their Chinese counterparts, and in these first years the Assams were very poorly made and harsh tasting. As trade boomed the clipper ships made their name, racing across the oceans with their harvest. Yet by the 1870s the tall ships were being supplanted by the faster, though more prosaic steamers. The last year in which China dominated tea imports to England was 1886. Black Indian or Empire teas have predominated ever since.

A number of English traders made their names in tea, many campaigning against the adulteration of tea, so common at the time: the Twining family; Horniman, from the Isle of Wight; the Jacksons of Piccadilly; and Scot Thomas Lipton. Lipton was an entrepreneurial grocer who made his name importing tea from Ceylon, as Sri Lanka was then known. Arriving after the coffee pest had ruined the coffee crop on which the island relied, he was able to buy up estates very cheaply and replant them to provide inexpensive tea for his shops back home. Lipton was a marketing wizard, and his product sold widely.

TWENTIETH-CENTURY TEA TRICKS

Iced tea

Tea merchant Richard Blechynden brought his wares to the 1904 World's Fair in St Louis. But he was plagued by the heatwave, which meant none of the visitors wanted to taste his hot teas. In desperation he put ice into his brewed tea and scored an instant hit. Today the USA consumes more iced tea than hot, though iced tea is only slowly invading that bastion of tea drinking, the UK. It takes time to overcome centuries of habit, though the climatic effects of El Niño and global warming may mean that the heatwaves will change all that.

Tea bags

Today the tea bag rules the world. It was invented in 1908 by New Yorker Thomas Sullivan, who stitched up his samples into little silk sachets. He soon realized just how convenient they were. In the intervening years the tea bag has gone through a number of tweaks, changing from square to round to pyramid-shaped and back again. There are all manner of complementary gadgets which hold used tea bags, or squeeze out the last drop. The little bag became a byword for the cheapest teas, the dust and fannings, which gave a quick strong

ICED TEA
Measure four teaspoons of tea into a six-cup pot and cover with cold water. Avoid brewing with boiling water like regular tea (this brings out too much tannin), as this can go cloudy when cool. Chill for four to six hours, then strain and serve, sweetening to taste. Serve in tall glasses with ice cubes and garnish with lemon slices and mint sprigs. Choose either a strong Ceylon, or a delicate Darjeeling.

brew. Today the bag has returned to its origins, with a few companies producing top quality teas in muslin bags.

Decaffeinated tea

Tea contains caffeine, which accounts for its refreshing, 'pick-me up' quality. There is no doubt that a thick brownish brew stewed in a large teapot will set the pulses racing. If you want tea without the kick, decaffeinated is available as leaves or tea bags. The caffeine is safely removed using methylene chloride, which leaves no residue. For a naturally caffeine-free infusion, a tisane is ideal – peppermint and camomile are particularly soothing. Remember that not all herbs are caffeine-free; Yerba Maté from South America contains more caffeine than coffee. However, if you are looking for a low caffeine tea, especially late at night, experiment with different teas. A lightly-brewed oolong tea will deliver less caffeine than a black tea, and a green tea less still. Or take a quality tea such as a Darjeeling and put only a few leaves into a delicate china dish and cover with boiling water. A fine black tea with a Chinese character responds well to this treatment. This is the kind of tea of which Jonathan Swift said:

Indeed, Madam, your ladyship is very sparing of your tea;
I protest the last I took was no more than water bewitched.

Instant tea

There's no doubt that tea leaves are messy, and you may choose to avoid leaves altogether by using granules. But don't try to pretend that instant and real have any similarities. And remember that by going for the fastest option you lose the chance of a few minutes' break from the stresses of daily life as you meditate over the kettle and the brewing leaves.

EYE SOOTHER
Restore sparkle to your weary eyes by placing cool stewed tea bags on closed eyelids. The relaxation is probably as beneficial as the bags, but it's worth a try.

TEA PLANTATIONS – at least the traditional unmechanized ones – are calm and serene places. Undulating over slopes and hills, the smooth lines are broken only by tall shade-giving trees. The shrubs are pruned, creating a flat, green table, three to four feet high. The only sounds rising from the bushes are the shrill voices of the women tea pickers in their brightly coloured clothes and the occasional distant hum of a van or tractor.

Tea bushes, like coffee bushes, take five years to develop but can then be harvested for the next fifty years. The flavour of the tea varies from day to day, depending on the weather as much as the general climate and the soil. A wet spell will promote more new growth. That's one of the reasons why blends are so important in tea: they assure consistency in a naturally erratic product.

There are over 2,000 varieties of tea. Like wine, teas vary substantially round the world, and even from valley to valley. Whether the tea bush is on a sunny slope or a shady one makes a real difference. Tea tasters can detect the amount of moisture on the day of picking – whether there had recently been monsoon rain or a dry spell.

All speciality teas are harvested by the traditional or 'orthodox' method. The tip and the top two leaves of the youngest shoots are picked. The pickers are traditionally women; each

❛ *The naming of teas is a difficult matter,*
  It isn't just one of your everyday games –
  Some might think you as mad as a hatter
 Should you tell them each goes by several names.
 For starters each tea in this world must belong
   To the families Black or Green or Oolong;
 Then look more closely at these family trees –
  Some include Indians along with Chinese. ❜

T.S. Eliot, *The Naming of Cats*

carries a wicker basket on her back supported by a strap running over her head. The tea is harvested continuously during the season, so the pickers will be retracing their steps many times over the year. Since the best teas in Darjeeling and Ceylon grow at altitudes of between 3,000 and 6,000 feet the pickers are sometimes working over steep and difficult terraced slopes. In Assam and much of Africa, where the terrain is much easier, a skilled picker can harvest up to 80 kg of fresh leaves a day.

In lower, flatter regions mechanized picking means that coarser leaves and stems are often picked along with the tenderest leaves. These leaves are then manufactured, cut, torn and crushed to create small particles which will brew quickly. Ideal for tea bags, C.T.C. (cut, torn and curled) tea is an unspoken spectre in the finest tea gardens.

But black, green or oolong? It is all in the processing.

The plump, moist, freshly picked leaves are spread out on vast trays in airy shaded rooms for up to twenty-four hours to wither. As the moisture evaporates the leaves shrivel, losing up to half their weight, until they are ready for the next stage: rolling. The leaves are rolled and twisted, lengthways, by huge rotary machines. (The finest teas are still hand-rolled, however.) Rolling breaks up the cells in the leaf and starts the process of oxidation, also known as fermentation, when the leaf turns a coppery orange, autumnal colour.

During fermentation the classic characteristics of the individual teas develop. Broadly, the longer the fermentation the deeper the flavour. To stop the fermentation the leaves are fired – heated to dry them and give them their distinctive black colour. The combination of withering, fermentation and firing is very skilled, since the moisture content of the leaves varies daily; under- or over-estimating any one of these stages will spoil the tea.

Finally the teas are graded and packed in foil-lined wooden chests ready for transport – in the case of Darjeeling, brought precariously down mountain roads decorated with grim signs about the mortal risks of dangerous driving.

WHAT DO THOSE LETTERS MEAN?

Indian teas are graded by leaf size, whether whole leaf or broken. The best teas are also graded according to quality, and how much 'tip' there is. 'Tippy' teas have to be hand picked and carefully processed.

The most confusing word in this classification is Pekoe (pronounced 'Pek-oh'). Orange Pekoe was popularized by Thomas Lipton for his Ceylon teas. 'Orange' has absolutely nothing to do with the fruit – it refers to the Royal House of Orange and was a quality term used by the early Dutch traders; it also refers to the coppery orange colour of the drying tea leaves. Pekoe comes from the Chinese for 'white hair' and means the downy tips of young leaves.

SFTGFOP
Special Finest Tippy Golden Flowery Orange Pekoe
The finest grade, with twists of leaf and plenty of tip.

TGFOP, FOP
Tippy Golden Flowery Orange Pekoe and Flowery Orange Pekoe
Quality long twists of leaf with a good amount of tip.

OP
Orange Pekoe
A large-leaf tea with whole rolled leaves but no tips.
Pekoe
A smaller grade of leaf.

GBOP, FBOP
Golden or Flowery Broken Orange Pekoe
Neat small leaf with plenty of pale tips.

BOP
Broken Orange Pekoe
A smaller leaf with no dust. Widely used for everyday teas.

BLACK TEAS

India

ASSAM The home of India's own wild *Camellia sinensis*, Assam's teas are grown in the fertile rolling hills of the vast Bramahputra River and the majority are rich and strong with small leaves – ideally suited for breakfast and for blends. The Assam first flush, usually picked in March, is a fairly astringent tea with the freshness of the new season. The smaller grades – Orange Fannings – are ideal for the notorious Irish Breakfast Tea, in which you are rumoured to be able to stand your spoon.

DARJEELING The tea estates in the foothills of the Himalayas are among the most picturesque in the world. The planters' bungalows are decorated with colourful shrubs, and their rolling green plantations lie in the dramatic shadows of the greatest mountains. The altitude, the cool air and the clean environment make for outstanding teas. Because of their altitude Darjeeling teas have very distinct seasons – and the higher up they are grown, the lighter the tea. The first flush, picked in April, is light and fragrant with a distinctive green character – a special treat for tea connoisseurs.

The second flush, the main crop, is classically described as having a muscatel flavour, which towards the end of the season develops a fruity flavour reminiscent of blackcurrant bushes. Darjeeling is known as the champagne of teas, and should never be swamped with milk. Like champagne it is an expensive drink, so expect to pay top prices for a named-estate Darjeeling, especially first flush. Blends are available containing at least 50 per cent Darjeeling, and these lower grades will take milk. Read the label very carefully and buy the best.

NILGIRI This black tea comes from the southern most tip of India. It's a lush, green hilly region, so produces teas very similar to those of its neighbour Ceylon; bright-tasting, clean, fresh, pleasantly strong, but lighter than Assam teas.

Sri Lanka

CEYLON The hilly region with its beautiful gardens in the south-west of this semi-tropical island has ideal conditions. Its extremes of climate help produce wonderful teas with remarkably different styles and tastes. The best teas come from the Uva district, which produces pale-coloured, slightly astringent teas. Dimbula produces classic coppery-coloured, stronger teas without Uva's astringency. Nuwara Eliya has beautiful gardens producing light, clean teas with plenty of flavour. The estates around the old capital Kandy, with its famous lake, grow a strong, smooth dark tea.

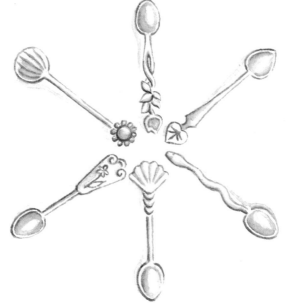

China

KEEMUN This is China's most famous black tea, and it comes from Anhwei Province. It was one of the first teas developed by the Chinese for the export market and was England's breakfast tea until Indian tea became available. The brew is smooth and slightly sweet with a distinct aroma of orchids.

China has a number of other black teas, most notably Yunnan and Szechuan Province. None of China's black teas are as robust as an Assam.

LAPSANG SOUCHONG This is the tea with the famous smoky aroma. Originally the flavouring came partly from bauxite in the soil and partly from drying the tea on tables covered by old fishing nets. The tarry, smoky flavour is added these days during the firing process. Chinese Lapsang is smoother and richer than Formosan, which has a character of burnt car tyres or tarmac roads on a hot day. Never make Lapsang too strong; a pinch in a pot really will do nicely. Lapsang is not as fashionable as it once was, though some cooks are beginning to experiment with it, as an aroma for scenting smoked foods, custards and ice creams.

Africa

Africa produces very large quantities of tea, especially for the tea-bag business. The best teas come from Kenya, Rwanda, Burundi and Zimbabwe. *Their* small leaf tea is particularly full bodied and quickly produces a good colour. It is the colour and richness of the teas that makes them ideal for tea bags, which depend on eye appeal. This quality also means they can easily be mistaken for coffee, especially if brewed for too long. That anyway was Mr Punch's view in 1902:

Look here Steward, if this is coffee, I want tea; but if this is tea, then I wish for coffee.

South America

The best sites in South America are usually given over to coffee. Maté is often preferred – an astringent leaf which is high in tannin and caffeine. Fairly standard tea-bag tea is grown in Argentina and Brazil.

Georgia and Turkey

These neighbouring states produce pleasant light teas, more like a Nilgiri or strong Keemun than an Assam.

Indonesia and Sumatra

While these regions are most famous for their coffees, they do produce tea. These are less astringent and flavoursome than Assams, and are used as a base for blending.

GREEN TEAS

These were the first teas to be enjoyed by the world, but they have been overtaken in the West by black teas. Perhaps it was the stresses of daily life that made a strong tea the blessing of the working classes. Or perhaps the pale, decorative elegance of the drink, without milk or sugar, was too subtle to accompany the Western diet.

Green teas are picked but neither withered nor fermented. The freshly picked leaves are simply rolled and then dried quickly, which prevents them going brown. The leaves are then sorted and graded. Certainly, a green tea, which can develop a distinctive bitter taste if made strong, can be an acquired taste. It is a brilliant digestif though, and the health benefits of green tea are beginning to be recognized by Western science. It is high in vitamin C, and contains a number of B vitamins, particularly folic acid, niacin, pantothenic acid and riboflavin. It is also rich in fluoride. Recent research suggests that it might be helpful in protecting against heart disease and some cancers.

China

GUNPOWDER So-called because it looked like the explosive substance that the early Western traders wanted to buy from the Chinese – a mass of grey-green tightly rolled balls. It produces a pale yellow-green liquor and has a refreshingly dry and astringent taste. Brew it lightly with only a few leaves or it will become bitter.

SILVER NEEDLE (WHITE TIP) This is tea made entirely of the finest silvery tips, which can only be picked from

specially cultivated bushes for a few days at the beginning of the season. The tea is not fermented or rolled, simply steamed dry. The pale yellow liquor from these unopened tips is very mild and smooth with a delicate sweet taste, making the drink an ideal digestif. One of the most famous white-tip teas was picked for the Emperor alone, and the stipulation was that the girls who did the picking had to be virgins.

Japan

MATCHA This is the powdered green tea that is used in the Japanese tea ceremony. It is brewed at 85°C in a very elaborate ceremony and is whisked to produce a frothy astringent drink that is rich in vitamin C.

SENCHA This is the most popular Japanese tea and is probably the purest of all green teas. The leaves are rolled and *steamed dry* immediately after picking. Again, do not brew this tea too strong.

OOLONG TEAS

Oolong means 'black dragon' in Chinese. It is a term for a tea that is 'semi-fermented', that is to say the leaves are withered and fermented very briefly. The leaves are shaken during fermentation to bruise them and speed up the process. The tea is then fired to the point where the luscious leaves develop peachy notes. Some of the best oolongs come from Formosa, today's Taiwan. Flower names are used for quality teas – Peony, White Rose, and Peach Blossom.

Drink oolongs Chinese style, placing a few leaves in a bowl and topping up with boiling water when necessary.

MONKEY-PICKED The world's best China oolong and a real curiosity. Wild tea which has seeded itself in crevices and on steep cliffs develops a heavenly fragrance and a delicate, exotic, dry yet warming character. Traditionally monkeys were trained to gather the leaves. Only a few pounds of this tea ever appear on the market at any one time.

BLENDED TEAS

ENGLISH BREAKFAST This classic was invented by a Scotsman a century ago, using black Indian and China teas to create a strong brew to drink with milk. Today's blend is stronger and contains Assam for strength, Ceylon for flavour and African for colour.

The British Isles have other 'regional' blends: Yorkshire Tea and Irish Breakfast Tea pay tribute to their populations' love of a good strong cuppa. They also reflect the quality of the water. Yorkshire and Irish water is soft, so it needs an Assam style. The Irish are devotees – they used to declare that the best tea went to China, the next best to Ireland and the poorest to England.

RUSSIAN CARAVAN The original Russian caravan was made up of China tea that had come to Europe by camel caravan on the silk and spice trade route across Russia. Today it is a blend of China tea – smooth, aromatic, and can be made strong enough to take milk.

FLAVOURED TEAS

The original flavoured teas go back centuries: the Indians and Arabs added spices, the Chinese added flowers, including jasmine, rose and chrysanthemum petals. Today teas are flavoured with an exotic range of nature identical flavourings. The market has grown from almost nothing in 1970, when blenders hesitantly added peach, apple and mango flavours. These seem restrained now compared with today's offerings of Summer Pudding, Apple Crumble, Irish Cream, and Sticky Toffee.

EARL GREY Perhaps the most famous, this was the first flavoured tea in the West and is a blend of Indian and China teas flavoured with oil

cold tea brandy (1693) **Scotch tea** whisky (1887) **a tea-bottle** an old maid with a fondness for tea **Tea Cake** a Forces' nickname for a man named Smith (twentieth century) **a tea-cup and saucer** a very respectable middle-class play (1865)	**tea-kettle purger (or a teapot)** a total abstainer (1909) **smash the teapot** break a pledge of abstinence (1909) **a teapot** a spooned stroke in cricket (1885) **to have one's teapot mended, or get it down the spout** in prison, to be restored to the privilege of tea (twentieth century)	**tea-leaf** thief (1905) **teaspoon** £5,000 (1860) **a cup of tea** ironic Cockney saying for someone slightly in the wrong - 'You're a nice ol' cup o' tea, ain't yer?' Eric Partridge, *A Dictionary of Slang and Unconventional English*

of bergamot, a small citrus fruit. The tea is named after Earl Grey (1764–1845) who was Prime Minister under William IV. The Earl Grey range has expanded, so that it is now possible to buy a selection of Earl Greys for different times of the day.

JASMINE This is a particularly delicious variation of green tea. The tea is scented with jasmine flowers, picked in the morning when the blossoms are closed and then added to the tea as they are about to open. Lightly brewed jasmine is always served with Chinese food.

ORGANIC TEAS

These are still hard to find. Yet many growers already produce organic teas, simply because they follow the old traditions and find it cheaper not to use pesticides. They do not register as organic because of the additional cost.

TISANES

Most drinkers come to discover herbal teas or tisanes for their medicinal benefits – for bringing sleep to the sleepless or calm to the unsettled stomach – or simply as a caffeine-free alternative.

The world divides into those who favour the classic varieties – such as peppermint and camomile and lemon verbena –

Great love affairs start with Champagne and end with tisane.

Honoré de Balzac

and those who indulge their passions with a wide range of colourful blends, containing fruit peels and flowers as well as herbs and spices. The blends are only limited by the creators' imaginations. Tisanes do not last as well as teas. This is definitely a case where it is best to buy little and often.

WHICH TEA SHALL I CHOOSE?

A refreshing tea with milk for breakfast:
Ceylon, English Breakfast
After-lunch digestif:
Mango, Peach
An afternoon reviver:
Earl Grey, Orange Pekoe, Darjeeling
Ideal with fruit cake:
strong Assam, mild Vanilla
Ideal with a fried breakfast:
Kenya, Assam
Bedtime soother:
Darjeeling, light China, Summer Pudding

THE PERFECT CUP

THE ELABORATE RITUAL of the Japanese tea ceremony never struck a chord in the West. Yet as you make your tea always linger a little over the moment. Make the best of the tea, but also enjoy the space and break from routine. Remember too that many speciality teas have very subtle differences that are easily ignored if you make the tea badly or drink it in haste.

1 Fill the kettle with freshly drawn cold water – let the tap run a little before you fill the kettle. Never use hot water from the tap. Filtered and bottled water are both less oxygenated than water straight from the tap; use them only if your tap water is very poor quality.

2 Warm the pot – or mug – with a dash of very hot water. This ensures the brewing temperature will be correct; if the pot is cold, this would reduce the temperature of the boiling water when it is poured in. Do this before the kettle has boiled – the water should only boil once.

3 Discard the hot water and measure in the tea. A tea bag contains 2.25g of tea, a teaspoon 5–8g.

4 Pour the water into the pot as it boils. Over-boiled water will have lost much of its oxygen and makes a very dull cup. Off-the-boil water will not be hot enough.

5 Leave to infuse for four to five minutes.

A great cup of tea does not stop at the kettle. The teapot is just as important. If you only drink strong Indian, Ceylon or African teas, then one pot is all you

MILK – BEFORE OR AFTER?

Tea is a drink riddled with rituals and this is one of the worst. Which is socially nicer? To be scientific for a moment, the correct way is to put the milk in first because the hot tea homogenizes the fats in the milk. However, this only works if you know exactly how strong your brew is and how much milk you will need. Pouring the tea first may have originated to show off the quality of one's china and the brew itself. In the earliest days of tea drinking in France, milk was put in first to help protect the fine porcelain from cracking on contact with the hot tea. There's an old Irish joke that says putting the milk in second is ideal if you have mislaid the tea strainer, because the milk pushes the leaves to the bottom of the cup.

The real question, well before MIF (milk-in-first) or MIS (milk-in-second), is why the West added milk to tea in the first place. After all, the first tea to come to Europe was green tea and the Chinese always drink it without milk. While black tea often goes well with milk, which needs a heavy tea to balance it, it simply does not settle comfortably with the light and fragrant Chinese and Japanese green teas.

	Number of teaspoons for a 6-cup pot	Milk	Strength 1 light to 4 strong
India:			
Darjeeling first flush	/	🍶 no	1
Darjeeling second flush	/ – //	🍶 optional	1
Darjeeling blends	// – ///	🍶 optional	2
Assam	/// – ////	🍶 yes	3
Nilgiri	// – ////	🍶 optional	2
Sri Lanka:			
Ceylon	/// – ////	🍶 yes	4
Orange Pekoe	// – ///	🍶 optional	3
Africa:			
Kenya	/// – ////	🍶 yes	4
China:			
Jasmine	/	🍶 no	1
Gunpowder	/	🍶 no	1
Yunnan	/ – ///	🍶 optional	2
Keemun	/ – ///	🍶 optional	2
Lapsang Souchong	/	🍶 no	1
Oolong	/	🍶 no	1
Japan:			
Sencha	/	🍶 no	1
Blends:			
English Breakfast	/// – ////	🍶 yes	4
Earl Grey	/ – ///	🍶 optional	2
Russian Caravan	// – ///	🍶 optional	2

Note Always infuse for five minutes. Chinese and Oolong teas can be topped up again and again with fresh boiling water, becoming progressively more diluted.

🍶 yes   🍶 optional   🍶 no

need. But if you also drink milder green Chinese teas, then you really need a separate pot. Finally if you like the highly perfumed teas and particularly enjoy Lapsang Souchong or Earl Grey then you should properly have a separate pot for them. Lovers of first-flush Darjeelings will certainly keep a pot for those.

If you want to experiment with the subtleties of teas treat yourself to three teapots. A strong black tea demands a good solid teapot, such as a Brown Betty. A China tea would blossom in a proper China teapot with a wicker handle and bowls rather than cups, while Lapsang or Earl Grey would appreciate the glamour of a traditional floral design. If it seems extravagant, then remember that fine wines demand glasses of different shapes: sherries, champagnes, clarets and brandies.

WHAT'S WRONG WITH MY TEA?

My tea tastes harsh and bitter
You have probably over-measured the tea. In general, you can always use less than you think you need. For a start, ignore the 'one for the pot' rule. Or you may have brewed it for too long. Teapots with a removable filter, or a cafetière-style plunger, are ideal.

My tea looks cloudy
This could be a good sign: quality Assams cream over and reflect the light. But if the tea is really cloudy then it is the water or a poor-quality tea and you need to try another variety.

My tea tastes metallic
This is usually a problem with the quality of the water, or the tea is of poor quality.

My tea looks scummy
Again, this is usually a water problem, as it is when the water clings to the side of the cup. It could be down to using poor-quality small-leaf tea, though. Experiment with bottled or filtered water.

My tea tastes dull and flat
This is because you are using poor-quality tea – treat yourself to something better. Or else you have reboiled the water, or let it go off the boil before pouring.

My tea is tasteless
You have probably stored it for too long. Buy little and often for a really good cup. This also gives you a chance to vary the teas you drink.

Glass teapots work as well as china; especially the ones that have a cafetière system where the leaves are isolated in the bottom of the pot after brewing.

Speciality teas do not have to be made in teapots. A tea sock – as unglamorous to look at as it sounds – works well because it fits any size of teapot and you can remove the leaves as soon as the tea is made. The range of quality teas made with real leaves in tea bags is still small, so this is a good option for one cup.

A China tea or a first-flush Darjeeling looks delicious in a porcelain cup or bowl without a handle, as it was first drunk.

> ❝ And suddenly the memory revealed itself. The taste was that of the little piece of madeleine which on Sunday morning at Combray (because on those mornings I did not go out before Mass), when I went to say good morning to her in her bedroom, my aunt Leonie used to give me, dipping it first in her own cup of tea or tisane. ❞
>
> Marcel Proust, *Du côté de chez Swann*

HOW TO STORE TEA

Well-made black teas can last for up to two years in a vacuum pack or sealed tin, though it can be difficult to find out just when the tea was harvested. Most teas travel by sea so that it takes some months for them to arrive in the shops. It is only possible to tell with teas grown in areas with marked seasons, such as Darjeeling which declares a first and second flush. For instance, a first flush sold in June will be about three months old. Delicate black teas like this will only last up to six months and that goes for green teas too.

Store the tea in a dark, airtight container with no risk of damp or condensation. Keep it well away from spices and strong-smelling foods as the tea will be tainted quickly. One London tea merchant bans workers from eating oranges and potato chips in the warehouse for that very reason.

THE PROFESSIONALS at work make an impressive display. A row of white china mugs is laid out on a long worktable. A busy broker may taste between 300 and 400 teas a day. It is an essential task because every day's picking will taste slightly different from the last (for no two days are the same with tea). The exact amount of leaves is weighed out of a small, paper sample packet on old-fashioned portable brass scales. The brewing mug is filled with water, the lid is put on and left to brew. After exactly five minutes the tea is poured into a small china bowl in front of the brewing mug.

The liquor glints in the bowls. As the taster walks fairly rapidly down the line he (for it is normally he) slurps and spits the teas, sliding towards him the bowls he likes and pushing away the ones he doesn't. He can then go back and taste his favourites. If the growers have come as a group to have their teas assessed by an expert then it's a moment of ritual humiliation as one person's tea is rejected while another's is acclaimed.

Five steps to bluff your way as a tea taster

1 Look at the leaves. Are they even-sized? How large/small are they? The larger the leaf the better the quality, unless it is top quality in which case you will be looking only for fine tips.

2 Smell the aroma of the liquor and of the wet leaves in the strainer. Was the aroma released as soon as the water was poured onto the leaves?

3 Look at the liquor. Is it fresh and bright, with a golden halo round the edge of the bowl or cup?

4 At last take a sip, and keeping the tea in your mouth suck in air through your teeth with a slurping noise. How much body does it have? How much tannin can you feel? Does the taste reflect the aroma?

5 Spit it out if you are tasting more than one or two.

Tea tasters rely on the classic if rather obscure vocabulary below. Practise developing your own, looking for characteristics, identifying flowery or fruity flavours.

Good	Bad	Good	Bad
flowery	soapy	pungent	sweaty
malty	dull	full body	thick
astringent	soft	fragrant	harsh
brisk	flat	bright	cloudy

TEA TERMINOLOGY

autumnal
Late-season tea from Assam and Darjeeling (September–October).

astringent
The technical term for the typically mouth-drying character of a green tea or a lightly fermented black tea. Not in the least derogatory.

burnt
The taste of tea that has been fired too long.

Bohea
Originally a black tea from China; in the eighteenth century the name for all tea. Familiar to readers of historical romances, whose heroines spend their lives dreaming of husbands over a dish (the earliest cups from China did not have handles) of Bohea.

bright
The clean fresh taste of a good tea.

brisk
Very popular with tea tasters, this one, if unintelligible to the rest of the world: the freshness of fresh tea.

chesty
A slightly dull, woody taste which some teas develop, which may be attributable to time spent in a tea chest, or poor picking and grading.

coloury
A bright attractive colour.

C.T.C.
Cut, torn and curled – tea leaves that have been machine processed for tea bags.

flush
A period of growth during the seasonal cycle of a tea bush growing in a region where there are marked seasons. The term is most commonly

used of Darjeeling's best teas; the first-flush tea is the first harvest of the year in February/March; the second flush starts in early April and is the main crop.

liquor
The term for brewed tea.

malty
A particular characteristic of Assam tea – like brewer's malt.

pungent
A positive word for clean fresh tea.

self-drinker
What the tea blender calls a tea that is good enough to be drunk by itself. It does not need blending.

tannin
Naturally present in all leaves and wood, it contributes to the dry taste in the mouth. Becomes bitter in a tea that has been dried too quickly.

TIME FOR TEA

WHEREVER IT IS DRUNK, tea has developed its own rituals, usually associated with delicious food. It may not be the drink of passion, but it is the drink of conversation.

6 Stands the Church clock at ten to three?
And is there honey still for tea? 9
Rupert Brooke, *The Old Vicarage, Grantchester*

In Egypt the tea will come in a glass on a metal tray, together with a glass of water and some sugar. In many Arab countries tea is the first sign of friendship and is drunk with intensely sweet pastries. In Russia, the strong tea of the samovar is soothed by a lump of sugar or a spoonful of jam. In France the custom has grown of drinking it in a languid fashion with delicate pastries.

Cardinal Mazarin introduced the tea habit to the French Court, since he was taking it for gout. For a long time tea drinking was a rare luxury, exclusive to the Court, involving the most precious tea services. Coffee, by contrast, was more accessible. When the first French teashops opened in the nineteenth century, they were the only places in which ladies could be seen without appearing 'fast'.

In England tea drinking rapidly became popular with all classes. In the late eighteenth century the London tea gardens at Ranelagh, Marylebone and Vauxhall became very fashionable. Here people could stroll and watch the entertainments, while enjoying cups of tea and bread and butter. Tea was also the mainstay of the temperance movement, which called the downtrodden to meetings where they were fed tea and sympathy.

For tea, though ridiculed by those who are naturally coarse in their nervous sensibilities, or are become so from wine-drinking, and are not susceptible of influence from so refined a stimulant, will always be the favoured beverage of the intellectual.
Thomas De Quincy,
Confessions of an English Opium Eater

The creation of 'tea time' resulted from the changing of the hours for dinner from four o'clock in the afternoon to seven or eight o'clock in the evening. Anna, Duchess of Bedford, is credited with introducing the ritual of tea in the early nineteenth century as a way of staving off hunger pangs.

This was also the heyday of the silver teapot, and all the associated paraphernalia of indulgence. In the big houses the servants would supply the hot water, but the lady of the house would make the tea. This was the meal that gave rise to the rule dreaded by all children – sandwiches before plain cake, plain cake before fruit cake, fruit cake before jelly.

READING THE LEAVES
Drain your cup, invert it into the saucer, and then turn upright again. (The symbolism is obvious, as you can see from these examples.)

Three small leaves close to a larger one mean a man.
Two small ones next to a smaller one mean a woman.
Small leaves in a triangle mean a child.
A heart shape means love, obviously, while a triangle means jealousy, and a key means secrets.

THREE MORE USES FOR TEA LEAVES

1 Put a few leaves in the water when boiling eggs. Try boiling some with green tea and some with black for variety.
2 Be sure to save brewed leaves for the compost bin.
3 Remember the tips of the Victorian era: cold stewed leaves were used to polish glasses and mirrors. Tea leaves boiled up in pans remove smells.

As for the workers, the tea break was instituted in 1820 to tide them over until they returned home hungry for their High Tea, a custom that still remains in the North of England, and in Scotland. It includes hot and cold foods, meat pies and cold meats, salads, plenty of bread and cheese and jam, followed by fruit loaves and cakes.

The first teashop in London opened in 1884, belonging to the ABC bakery, which was soon followed by the Express Dairy, J. Lyons and Kardomah. Hot on their heels came the afternoon *thé dansant* or tea dance, where unaccompanied ladies could always find a debonair companion to twirl them to the tunes of the Palm Court Orchestra. Today the cup of tea is still fundamental, at Buckingham Palace garden parties, village cricket matches and at church bazaars everywhere.

COFFEE

❝ *Coffee, which makes the politician wise,*
And see through all things with his half-shut eyes. ❞

Alexander Pope, *The Rape of the Lock*

COFFEE: IT IS A call to action – the paper-cup latte of the early-to-work; the milky libation of the coffee morning; the jumpstart after a good lunch; the unction of the worldwide chatter in the cyber café; the lubricant of great thoughts and good conversation; and the late-night salute to the digestion. Whoever could dream of sleep after a cup? Where tea is the drink for calmness in crises, coffee is the friend of celebration.

All of this and more from a humble bean. But it is not until the bean is roasted that it becomes the drink that sets the world alight. It's the swishing bean in the roasting drum and the intense aroma of the release of the coffee oils that seduce the appetite and alert the brain.

Let's be honest, when it comes to sex appeal, coffee beats tea every time. It's impossible to be passionate over a cup of even the finest Darjeeling. Philosophical, yes, but passionate, no. Coffee keeps the love affair alight, while tea consoles the abandoned. To give spice to your love life discover the world of coffees, and then the infinite variety of roasts and grinds and machines to make your brew.

In the wild, coffee grows as a charming and decorative tree, easily sixty feet high, though on the farms and estates where it is cultivated today it is kept down to a simple six-foot bush. The long skinny branches miraculously boast shiny green leaves, tiny jasmine-scented blossoms and clusters of cherries, green and rosy ripe, all at the same time.

Inside each cherry are two coffee beans tucked together, flat sides facing, protected from the pulp of the fruit by layers of 'parchment'. The great mystery is how it was discovered that the cherries merited processing

into a drink. Even then it took 600 years from the first records of the coffee cherry before brewing coffee was properly understood, and another 500 years before filtering coffee was invented. As for named coffees, from identified countries, they only came to be marketed 200 years ago, and it was only just over fifty years ago that the first commercial espresso machine was introduced.

IT BEGAN WITH THE GOATS

So who did discover the joy of coffee for the world? One story has it that the benefit of the bean was discovered by Kaldi, an Abyssinian goatherd, who found his flock was friskier after eating the fruits. In his turn the local holy man welcomed the way the cherries kept him awake through long sessions of prayer.

There's another story that a holy man, Ali bin Omar al-Shadhili, was found guilty of forming a relationship with the king's daughter. As a result he was banished to the Yemen, where he and his disciples ate the berries, and cooked them and drank the liquid. They subsequently cured the king's people of a sickness by giving them coffee to drink. Al-Shadhili was pardoned, and won an everlasting place in the pantheon as patron saint of coffee growers and coffee drinkers.

Whatever the truth of these stories, it is known that the best of beans, the Arabica, originates in the Red Sea area, and that beans may have been cultivated as far back as the sixth century. In the very earliest days the fruit continued to be eaten whole, or it was crushed to a paste with fat, or drunk as a soupy stew of the cherry – pulp, bean and all. It was not until about the thirteenth century that coffee was roasted and became more like the drink that we know today – at least in the countries of the Middle East.

As the rest of the world began to discover the stimulating properties of *kahwa*, as it was then called, the passion for it became intense, and spread rapidly. There are some ripping yarns of bravery and theft as individuals attempted to steal the coffee seeds; only the cleaned beans were sold to prevent people from growing their own. Baba Budan, a Moslem pilgrim, tied seven legendary seeds to his belly and smuggled them out of Arabia to south India. The descendants of the original plants are still growing today, because of the fortunate fact that the coffee tree is self-pollinating. As a result it is also free from mutation.

The Dutch took the South Indian coffees on to Java. At one time the Mocha-Java blend represented the whole world of coffee growing (Mocha being the name for coffees from Ethiopia and the Yemen). Louis XIV was naturally impatient to own the beans and so the Dutch gave him a tree that he kept in a special glasshouse in Versailles. This effectively became the parent of the coffee industry today, for cuttings from this tree were taken to Martinique by the Chevalier Gabriel de Clieu in the 1720s, a key character in what Kenneth Davids cheerfully calls the 'kinky karma of coffee'. The Chevalier's cuttings were attacked

by another traveller on the ship and later, when the ship was becalmed, all but one of the cuttings died. The Chevalier kept the survivor alive by sharing his own dwindling water supply with it.

To good effect: fifty years later there were nearly 19 million trees on Martinique and the cultivation of the trees had spread across the Caribbean from the single seedling. Some shoots were also sent to Réunion, in the Indian Ocean, then known as the Isle of Bourbon; this was a variety of Arabica developed as smaller beans, which became known as the Bourbon. This is the bean grown in Brazil for the Santos coffees, and for the Oaxaca coffees of Mexico.

Brazil has its own hero of coffee: Francisco de Melho Palheta, who was sent to French Guyana to find seeds. He had no success until he turned on his Latin charms and wooed the wife of the Governor. She sent him some coffee-bean cuttings concealed inside a bouquet of flowers. Some 250 years later Brazil is the largest producer of coffee in the world.

Finally, at the end of the nineteenth century the coffee bean completed its circle of the globe when seeds were introduced into Kenya and Tanganyika, some few hundred miles south of their original home in Ethiopia. These were ideal new sites at a time when many of the world's original estates had recently been wiped out by disease, much as phylloxera devastated the vine. Coffee could only survive on high ground, which these countries provided.

Since then the world has recovered from the destruction of plants and coffee is thriving everywhere, most recently and successfully in Australia.

FROM COFFEE HOUSE TO COFFEE BAR

I T TOOK 600 YEARS for the world to learn how to brew a palatable cup, and coffee houses were also slow off the mark. The first one opened in Cairo as late as 1550. Coffee soon became a challenge to established religion, and coffee houses rapidly became known as places of subversion. In a number of centres across the Middle East coffee houses were attacked and closed down. The fiercest attack on coffee drinkers was by a Grand Vizir of Constantinople around 1600. The worst offenders were sewn up in leather bags and thrown in the Bosphorus.

In Europe coffee brought the same trail of infamous behaviour by providing places for men to meet. Women joined governments in their disapproval, and in 1674 a Women's Petition Against Coffee denounced the brew for the way it enticed men away from their homes.

Coffee arrived in Venice, one of the gateways to Europe, within five years of the arrival of tea, and less than a century after chocolate. These delicious drinks, the last perhaps more deliciously sinful than the rest, became fundamental to daily life. Initially they had all been drunk unsweetened but as the fashion for these drinks grew the consumption of sugar boomed (a great benefit to the plantation owners) and has never fallen since. It is hard to imagine the excitement of these drinks, especially as they arrived so closely upon one other; drinks so important that they created customs and cultures of their own.

One of coffee's heroes in Europe is Franz Kolchitsky. It is well known that Vienna's pastry cooks invented croissants, representing the Turks' crescent flag, to celebrate the end of the Turkish siege of the city. However, the Turks themselves left behind an important gift – sacks of coffee. Kolchitsky had been a prisoner of war and was able to explain what the beans were intended for. The Viennese public needed some persuasion – with sugar and cream – but it quickly became a habit.

In London the coffee houses were once known as penny universities – you paid a penny to enter and two pennies for the coffee and a paper. They were the places to find out the news and pass it on, to such an extent that the coffee houses of London made a bid to run the monopoly of the newspapers. The government of the day soon stamped on that, and coffee gradually found itself supplanted by the far less subversive tea.

In the United States, of course, it was an entirely different story. The Boston Tea Party put a resounding end to tea drinking. Little did the protesters in the harbour that December 1773 evening realize that a consequence of their throwing 340 tea chests into the water would be to give rise to a national habit for mild-roast coffees.

> The Boston Tea Party should have been called the Boston Coffee Morning, since it prompted America to turn its back on the black and green leaves and embrace the shiny bean.

The cafés of France started to grow with the arrival from Sicily of Francisco Procopio. He watched the success of Vienna's coffee houses and started up his own at Café Procope at the end of the eighteenth century. Here you could buy coffee, yes, but also sorbets and sweetmeats, as well as alcoholic drinks, and you could read the papers and play chess.

In the heyday of the European coffee house, they were places open to the world. The caffeine gave the stimulus to clear thought and argument; the ale house was quite the opposite. No wonder some well-known revolutions were fomented in coffee houses – you had to be sober enough to work out the detail. It was at the back of one coffee house that Edward Lloyd began to insure cargoes for the Indies, and the Baltic Exchange and the Commercial Union similarly had their beginnings in such places.

The coffee houses lay at the heart of the Age of Reason, which ran from the English revolution of 1688 to the French Revolution in 1789 – so say the Illy brothers in *The Book of Coffee*.

Voltaire (1694–1778) was said to have consumed fifty cups of coffee a day.

coffee-mill
mouth (1800)
coffee pot
a small tank engine
(late 1900s)
coffee-shop
a coffin (1880)
coffee stall
a landing-craft kitchen,
supplying meals to small craft
off the Normandy beaches
(1944)

Eric Partridge,
*A Dictionary of Slang and
Unconventional English*

NAME YOUR DRINK

espresso
A single cup of espresso coffee, drunk black, often with sugar.
At its very best made from beans ground only an instant before,
and the base for the drinks below.

double espresso/espresso doppio
Twice the size, to jumpstart the day.

cappuccino
One-third espresso, two-thirds hot milk, heated up with steam.
In Italy a morning drink, and definitely not to be ordered after a meal as the
rest of the world does. Said to be named after the creamy-coloured
hoods of the Capuchin friars.

**café latte/café au lait/
café con leche**
One part espresso and two or three parts of foamed milk.

cafe corretto
An espresso with a dash of Sambuca or other spirit.

espresso macchiato
An espresso 'marked' with a dash of hot milk.

latte macchiato
A large glass of milk 'marked' with a shot of espresso.

espresso con panna
An espresso with whipped cream.

espresso ristretto
An espresso with less water than usual.

THE 1990s COFFEE BAR

Single
A shot of espresso.

Double
Two shots of espresso.

Short
Any style espresso drink (single or double) in a smallish cup.

Tall
In a medium cup.

Grande
In a large cup.

Skinny
With non-fat milk.

Dry
A cappuccino with no liquid milk, just foam.

Wet
A cappuccino with a small amount of milk as well as foam.

No fun
Decaffeinated.

With wings
To take away.

The next great change was a hundred years later: the invention of the espresso machine. As this masterpiece of steam engineering was refined it spread its influence. The arrival of the espresso machine in the UK caused a stir, if only short-lived. For a brief time, the boys with their slicked back hair and the girls with their full skirts murmured sweet nothings over a cheap cup. However they say the British did not know how to service their espresso machines, which is why the coffee bars disappeared so suddenly until the American chains burst on the scene some twenty years later.

In the meantime the coffee shops arrived. These tempting words suggest emporia selling coffee. Nothing could be further from the truth. Coffee shops were featureless lounges in hotels, airports and stations, wherever people were in transit. They served bland drinks and blander foods.

A warm welcome, then, to the American chains, originally from Seattle, which introduced drinkers who were afraid of espresso and its caffeine ratings to the fun of the steam machine. Coffee houses in northern Europe have become once more the temples of pleasure they have always been in the southern Mediterranean.

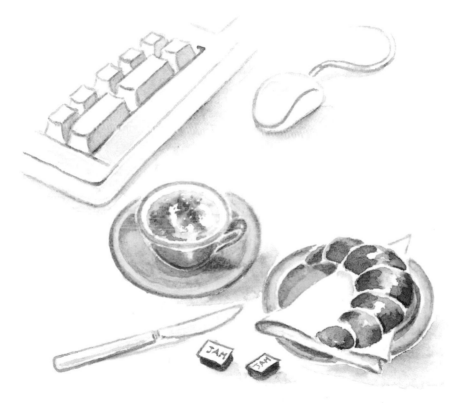

Coffee is the drink for the adventurous – if you want to see it growing, that is. It flourishes in tropical climates, often on distant mountainsides over 3,000 feet (900 m) high. Like the buyers, you risk having to contend with wars, coups, drug barons and rapidly fluctuating exchange rates.

A visit reveals that the work that goes into a cup is painstaking. While, increasingly, trees grown on flat land can be machine harvested, the disadvantage is that the machine removes all the fruit without discrimination – the unready and the ripe. If the fruit is not quickly and carefully sorted then there is a risk of contaminating the whole crop with a sour or bitter taste from unripe or spoiled fruits. Speciality

coffees, however, are hand picked and the trees have to be picked over a number of times in the season to select only the ripest cherries.

Each tree – six feet (1.8 m) tall yields 5 kg (11 lb) of coffee cherries every year, containing 2 kg (4 lb 4 oz) of coffee beans, which reduce to about 1½ kg (3 lb 3 oz) after roasting.

Each cup contains 6 g (¼ oz) of beans, which means each tree produces enough for 250 cups.

Inside the coffee cherry the two flat-sided beans – or sometimes just one 'Peaberry' bean – are covered in a layer of thin parchment, and then an outer membrane to protect them from the outer pulp of the cherry. The sweet flesh – which is very popular with monkeys – and the membrane have to be removed, and this has to be done quickly or the fruit will rot. The simplest method is the Dry Method, used in hot countries where there is little water. The cherries are laid out in the sun to dry for seven to ten days and raked regularly so they dry evenly. When dry, the cherries are beaten to remove the dried-up pulp. Any remaining parchment will come off in the roasting. These beans are called 'Naturals' and develop quite a spicy tang. Ethiopian Mocha, for instance, is still made by this method.

The Wet Method is more common in mountainous regions where there is plenty of water. Here the cherries are pulped to loosen the skins and then

soaked in water. In the warmth and the wet the cherries soon start to ferment. The beans are stirred with paddles and in two days the skins can simply be washed away. These 'washed coffees' are then laid out to dry in the sun and are raked over regularly. The final protective parchment is rubbed off at the mill and the beans given a special polish to make them look appealing. The great benefit of this method is that it is fast and the cleaned beans stay whole with less damage and retain their quality taste. The disadvantage is that it is labour intensive and demands large quantities of water.

Once processed by either method dry beans are picked over to remove the debris and graded according to shape and size by a series of sieves.

They are then labelled with their source, grade and how they were processed, and packed into their distinctive sacks. The person who brings the coffees to market is the broker, the key figure in the supply chain. Coffee is a commodity that remains fairly consistent in quality, certainly compared to tea.

That is why it has its own futures markets where traders can buy stocks in advance and speculate on the forward price of the bean. The Arabica – quality – market is in New York; the Robusta market is in London. The existence of these markets can hit small Third-World growers because it fixes the price of coffee artificially high or low.

CAFÉ DO
BRASIL

THE WORLD OF COFFEE

The most important aspect of coffee is what French wine growers call *terroir*, the unique combination of climate, soil and geographical position. The effects of *terroir* in wine are much argued, but in coffees there's no doubt that low-grown coffees don't taste as fine as the higher-grown ones.

What makes the difference is where in the the world your coffee was grown. Coffees vary from country to country, from region to region. Exactly like wine, there are different species of bush, and enormous variations in soil and climate. There is, however, a very general rule of thumb, which can be applied to the most important producing continents.

THE IMPORTANCE OF ISLAND-GROWN COFFEE

Coffee grows in some of the most exotic parts of the world, in particular on tropical islands created by volcanic activity. The rich soil, steamy climate and natural leaf compost are perfect.

The only negative factor could be the heat. Fortunately, the cloud cover, which accumulates during the day, provides a mid-afternoon drenching for the vegetation, and shades the bushes from the direct rays of the sun.

African coffees are generally spicy and bright, with a very good level of 'coffee acidity'. Their 'point' or piquant flavour will hit the tip of your tongue. It is therefore true to say that Kenya, Mocha and Tanzania will all have hints of the same spicy tang. South and Central American coffees are altogether smooth, suave and elegant, with lovely hints of nuttiness. Indonesian coffees are the heavyweights of the coffee world. They are rich, rounded and most exotic, with dramatic aromas of hazy tobacco and aromatic tropical spices. They have a flavour full enough to support milk, have a good balance of acidity and are usually served French-roasted.

Mass-market coffees will be blends, origin often unspecified. Some quality coffees are sold simply under their country of origin (i.e. 'Costa Rican'). Speciality coffees usually have a specific regional descriptor (e.g. 'Costa Rican Tres Rios'). But even that regional label gives nothing of the accuracy of wine labelling, which may be specific to the town and the river bank.

Part of the difficulty lies with land ownership. Many growers are simply small farmers who produce in minute quantities, often joining together with other local growers to sell to brokers and millers. There are few coffee estates as large as those tea estates in Darjeeling or Assam, so it is difficult to build a market for single-estate coffees.

Coffea Arabica is the variety that came from the Yemen and is the coffee of the highest quality. *Coffea Robusta* came from the Congo, and it is a sturdier, high-yielding plant. The quality is not so good, but its great advantage is that it grows easily and uncomplainingly almost anywhere, and it can be used in blends or to make instant coffee.

One quality descriptor to look for is 'hard', because the harder the bean the better it is, and the higher the altitude the coffee grows, the harder it is. Guatemalan labelled as 'hard' will not be quite as delicious as 'strictly hard'. How do you find out which is which? A coffee buyer can tell by sight the altitude at which the bean is grown, for a low-grown bean grows faster and its split is off-centre. For consumers the best way is to ask the retailer and learn by tasting. Another descriptor is AA, used on some African beans to indicate the best large bean; next are AB and B, which are smaller but whole beans.

It is worth noting that although most beans are the same shape and size, there are several exceptions, which some countries sort out and sell separately. Kenya is particularly good at this.

Peaberry Where only one round bean is formed in the cherry then it is a Peaberry. It is sought after because it has a more concentrated flavour than the two separate beans, and it roasts more evenly because it is round.

Elephant Ears Another curiosity, where one bean wraps itself round the other inside the cherry. They separate during roasting, creating a very definite ear shape. This larger bean can usually tolerate a darker roast.

Maragogype Pronounced 'Marago jeep', these beans are twice the normal size. This is a specific species, named after a town in Brazil where the bush was found. Other species do produce 'Elephant' grade beans but only at random. The best Maragogype for intensity of flavour comes from Guatemala; Nicaragua is also good.

Africa

MOCHA The mother of all Arabica coffees. The name has also come to mean coffee flavour, for chocolate flavour, and also a type of espresso.

STRENGTHS OF COFFEE

Every coffee has a different taste, depending on its origins. The strength, however, is determined by the level of roast. (Strong coffee is never to be brewed using more coffee; it will merely become thicker and heavier.)

High Continental Roast
STRENGTH 8
The strongest, blackest, shiniest roast, marvellous for espresso and cappuccino with a kick.

Light Continental Roast
STRENGTH 7
Dark, strong and smooth for milder espresso.

French Roast
STRENGTH 6
Dark brown, with a hint of the gloss of natural oils; smooth without bitterness.

Medium Roast
STRENGTH 5
A regular 'English Roast' that brings out the natural coffee flavours.

Mild Roast
STRENGTH 3
Light roast for a balanced gentle character.

Mocha develops a unique flavour from the time it spends maturing in the sun. It is one that is best described as winey and gamey. Given that the brew has a distinctively thin body, it is a drink with powerful attitude which some prefer to soften by blending, often with the second-oldest coffee in the world, Mysore, from Southern India. Even a small amount of Mocha in a blend will add a definite richness.
Strength **6**

KENYA At its best it is distinctively rich and aromatic, with pronounced coffee acidity, but not as challenging as Mocha. Usually sold medium roast; its natural acidity would turn sour if high roast. Certain Kenyan coffees are so spicy they curdle milk. The better coffees come from the slopes of Mounts Kenya and Elgon, and are graded from top quality downwards: AA, AB, B.
Strength **5**

More recently Kenya has been growing some of its own Blue Mountain coffee from plants imported from Jamaica. Very quickly the influence of climate and soil take over; any semblance of Blue Mountain is suppressed by the Kenyan character.
Strength **6**

TANZANIA Tanzania shares many similarities with Kenya, in history and in coffee. The best Arabica beans come from the mountain slopes and are graded AA and so on. Of the well-known names Chagga is a growers' group; Mbeya, Moshi and Arusha are towns. Milder than Kenyan, and can tolerate a darker roast. Work in recent years on planting and processing is paying off in terms of quality coffees. Strength **5**

All of the central African states, including Burundi, Cameroon, Malawi, Uganda, Rwanda, Zambia and Zaire, also grow a little Arabica and lots of Robusta.

Jamaica

There is more Jamaican Blue Mountain sold than there are trees to create the bean. But this is one area where there are named estates to look out for: Wallenford, Mavis Bank, Silver Fern. The best Blue Mountain, benefiting from volcanic soils, has a full body and sweet flavour with only moderate acidity. No wonder it has become the Bordeaux of coffees. But, like Bordeaux, it has also become staid. Obscurely exotic beans promise much more fun. Espresso drinkers certainly don't need it, because it does not benefit from a high roast, while cappuccino drinkers need a bolder coffee to dominate the milk. Blue Mountain is a mild coffee; don't try to drink this strong. Strength **2**

Dominican Republic and Haiti

Careful work in the Dominican Republic to control planting, harvesting and processing, and to take advantage of a superb humid climate and fertile volcanic soil is producing some excellent quality coffees. Haiti has

its own special classification system for its small output of Arabica, its best product being 'strictly high grown washed'. These both produce medium-bodied, rich, flavoursome coffee, which is French-roasted to bring out the best.
Strength **6**

Central and South America

MEXICO Coffees from Mexico have much in common with those from Brazil; they are generally light and mild. The best Mexican coffees come from the south. Look out for Coatepec, Huatusco and Orizaba, which are richer and stronger.
Strength **3**

GUATEMALA The wild forests on steep volcanic slopes are the home of the high grown 'strictly hard bean', the top quality coffees which have full body and acidity. There are delightfully warming hints of honey and black chocolate in the best Guatemalan. Look for beans from Antigua, Atitlan and Coban.
Strength **5**

NICARAGUA The climate and dramatic mountainous terrain places Nicaragua alongside Guatemala as a producer of excellent coffee. A rich, spicy and powerful coffee.
Strength **6**

COSTA RICA Full-bodied, full of flavour, much-prized coffees. Top districts are Heredia, Tarazu and Tres Rios. Costa Rica also uses the 'strictly hard bean' classification for its top beans. Medium roasting brings out a perfectly balanced coffee with the right aroma, body and

flavour, and the typical spicy notes. A good starting point against which to measure coffees from round the world.
Strength **3**

COLOMBIA Colombia is the world's most important grower of quality large Arabica beans and second only to Brazil in volume of production. It is a pity the intense marketing of instant coffee has helped debase the name of Colombia. It has become renowned for mild coffee. Colombia's top quality beans take a medium to high roast, creating a well-flavoured coffee with more intensity than some other Central American coffees. Top grade is supremo. The best are Armenia, Medellin and Manizales, and Bogotá and Buaramanga. Some of the original *Coffea Typica* is still grown way down south in the Andes around the towns of Popayan and Pitilito. It is richer, smoother, with a more concentrated flavour.
Strength **6**

BRAZIL The largest producer in the world. When there is a catastrophic frost in Brazil, the whole world of consumers knows it as prices soar. Its mass-market coffees are ideal for blending as they give body and smoothness at a good price. The quality coffee of Brazil is grown in Santos using the Bourbon seed that was originally imported from La Réunion, so it is a slightly different variety from the rest of America. A generally light and mild, medium-bodied coffee with a good aroma, which makes it ideal for daytime drinking.
Strength **3**

THE COFFEE TASTER'S VOCABULARY

Acidity A classic piece of coffee-taster's jargon, it is impenetrable to the rest of the world. If a coffee has acidity they say that it has 'point', that it has a bright, fresh taste, essential to some extent in all coffees. This has nothing to do with the pejorative meaning of sour acidity. Kenyan coffees are renowned for their acidity in contrast to the more mellow acidity in Central American coffees.

Body This is easier to follow – it is the same word that wine tasters use. It describes the mouth feel of the coffee, whether it is dense or thin. (This is assuming that the coffee has been correctly brewed and that any thickness is not just coming from sediment.)

Aroma There is a wide vocabulary to draw on, from nuts, smoke and wood, to earthy notes. A coffee with high acidity will have a more pronounced aroma.

Flavour This again has a wide vocabulary and will be determined by the combination of acidity, body and aroma, reflecting the very distinct differences across the world.

....

The professional taster uses several categories to describe coffees, with a range of descriptors:

Category	Description
Type of bean	Robusta, Arabica, washed or dry process
Taste	strictly soft ↔ harsh
Body	lacking ↔ too heavy
Acidity	some ↔ too much
Age	old ↔ fresh
Defects	sour, grassy, musty
Cup	roast, watery, burned, old
Overall assessment	neutral, spicy, hard
Fullness	slight ↔ considerable

Indonesia and South East Asia

The quality coffees of Indonesia are among the best in the world, with a flavour full enough to support milk. They have a good balance of acidity and are usually served French-roasted. They are languid, laid-back beans, the hammock-swingers of the coffee world.

SUMATRA The best coffees are Ankola, Blue (meaning best quality, and referring to the bluish tinge to the bean) Lintong and Mandheling, all grown in the volcanic highlands around lake Toba in the north. Smooth, sweet and intense without the nutty spiciness of Colombian. Strength **6**

A real curiosity of Sumatra lies on the verges of rumour and imagination. A small palm civit (a wildcat), the luak, eats the coffee cherries. It digests the flesh of the cherry but not the beans, which are later gathered. The coffee has a very distinctive taste much prized by collectors. In theory, such coffees can be found the world over wherever animals eat the cherries, but Kopi Luak coffee has become the most notorious.

JAVA One of the world's great coffees, it has beautiful long, flat beans, too large to become scorched or harsh if high roasted. There is an intense flavour and appealing dry earthiness in a good French-roast Java. Aged Java is available at a few select merchants. In times past it was stored for as much as several years in warehouses to mature, over time losing acidity and acquiring sweetness, along with the name Old Brown Java. Today the beans are stored in underground pits to develop the typically rich, mature flavour, and then dark roasted. Strength **6**

SULAWESI (CELEBES) To the buyers the coffee from Sulawesi is still known by its old name Celebes. And Kalosi is the bean they are chasing, grown by the local Toraja tribe in the rainforest around the highland town of the same name. Given a dark roast it develops spicy and nutty tones with plenty of smoky aromas. Definitely the surprise gift to put in the foot of a coffee drinker's Christmas stocking.
Strength **6**

PAPUA NEW GUINEA Papua New Guinea is a wild, untamed country, and a hint of that character shows in its coffee. Not yet as good as the other coffees from the area, but with many of their best qualities. An immense amount of work by Australians has lifted the quality of their Arabica. Look for Arona Valley.
Strength **5**

BALI Here's a romantic spot for coffee bushes, clinging onto the slopes of extinct volcanoes amongst the remaining mature forest, and they flourish on the island's volcanic soil. There is much more Robusta coffee in the low- lands, but the small quantities of Arabica in the hills make a rich dark roast.
Strength **6**

United States of America

HAWAII And here's another romantic spot. The coffee grows in the volcanic Kona district. Kona Hawaiian is rated by the Americans as the world's most luxurious coffee; just as the British see Jamaican Blue Mountain. Arabica bushes were brought from Brazil in 1818. Kona is medium roast and a fraction fuller than Blue Mountain, with which it

has a lot in common. It has the the particular sweetness of an island coffee. Kona is rich, smooth, gently nutty, gently spicy. It is not grown in any quantity and output is declining.
Strength **4**

India

MYSORE The state in southern India whither Baba Budan brought his smuggled seeds in the seventeenth century. The best regular Mysore is grown in the Coorg and Nilgiri Hills (also known for tea). Mysore is not often sold on its own, because it is remarkably mild. The most famous Indian coffee is Malabar. This is sold as Monsoon or Monsooned Malabar, which describes its ageing by exposure to the moist monsoon winds. This replicates the earlier effect on the coffee of a nine-month journey by sea to England. In the process the beans lose their acidity and mellow, and can be high roasted without acquiring the bite that black coffees can so often have.
Strength **7**

China

YUNNAN China has leapt into the world coffee market with huge volumes of bulk Arabica coffee, so it is difficult to identify any regional specialities. Medium-roast Yunnan has a clean, fresh taste, a little like Central American.
Strength **4**

Blends

There is a long tradition of blending coffees. Sometimes this is to keep the price down by mixing quality Arabicas with cheaper Robusta beans. Or it may be to create a more appealing blend by making it richer or more mellow. Blending also evens out inconsistencies in supply or quality for retailers who are looking to create their own house styles.

Kenya, Colombia and Costa Rica are all good candidates for blending, and they marry well with stronger coffees such as Mocha and Java.

MOCHA AND MYSORE This classic blend of the two oldest coffees in the world was being enjoyed in the 1600s. As recently as the 1970s it was being promoted as the 'perfect coffee for the proud hostess'. This is sales speak for a medium roast. There's good reason for the blend's popularity – the Mysore softens the Mocha's fiercest characteristics and gives it a fuller body.
Strength **5**

SANTOS AND JAVA Another popular blend, although with a shorter pedigree. In this case the hard clean-tasting Santos from Brazil is softened by the smooth dark velvety texture of Java. With a continental high roast it takes milk well and is ideal for smooth espresso and brilliant cappuccino.
Strength **7**

AFTER DINNER Read the small print: every producer has their own slightly different blend. A typical choice might be half Colombian and half Brazilian Santos, which is then roasted as dark as possible. A blend like this can tolerate a dark roast without becoming bitter. This roast is too dark to take milk well – the coffee will turn the depressing colour of dinner-party grey.
Strength **8**

BREAKFAST BLEND The aim here is to produce a coffee for non-espresso drinkers, which is rich and strong, and able to take milk, but does not need a continental roast. A typical blend might be Colombia and Ethiopia Mocha since the Colombian gives richness and body to the Mocha, and is just a little stronger than Mocha Mysore. Strength **6**

DECAFFEINATED COFFEE

If you want decaffeinated coffee, then there are two ways to remove the stimulus from the bean. In the first, the raw bean is steamed to expand it and the caffeine is then removed by the solvent methylene chloride. The bean is steamed clean to remove any traces, dried and then roasted as usual. This chemical is chosen because it is very volatile and evaporates at low temperatures, so that no traces, or only the minutest, are left. The second method of removal is a patented water process in which the bean is soaked in water to remove everything. The caffeine is removed, and all other elements are then re-introduced to the bean. Either way decaffeinated beans have their critics on flavour grounds.

There are other ways of enjoying coffee while cutting back on the caffeine. For instance, Arabica coffee contains less caffeine than Robusta, and the higher up the mountain the beans are grown the less caffeine they contain. So simply buy the best beans and you will be cutting back on the caffeine. High-roast coffees, strong though they taste, also have less caffeine because it has been lost in the roasting process, so buy French and Continental roasts rather than the medium breakfast variety.

Also experiment with your own blends; take a top quality low-caffeine bean (e.g. French-roast Colombian or Indonesian) and blend it with a good quality decaffeinated bean.

FLAVOURED COFFEES

The trend in exotics such as Chocolate Fudge flavoured coffee started in North America but it has yet to convert the traditional Mediterranean countries, though it is having success in Northern Europe. If you find the coffees too strong, try using flavoured syrups which many coffee shops sell. Or follow the well-tried route and stay with the flavourings enjoyed by the earliest drinkers in the Middle East, such as cardamom and cinnamon.

INSTANT COFFEE

This has to be one of the fastest of convenience drinks. Robusta coffee is most often used because it is strong enough to cope with the process and still produce a taste. The roasted ground coffee is brewed very strong in huge pressure machines and the liquor freeze-dried or dehydrated. It is possible to make an instant using good Arabica, but because price comes before quality, it is better to think of instant just as a pleasant drink, and not associate it with real coffee. But if it's flavour along with speed and convenience you seek, then think again – of a coffee sock. Or if it's for several people – a cafetière. In the UK, however, the pleasure of real beans is a well-kept secret, since 84 per cent of the coffee drunk is instant. In Germany meanwhile, it is the reverse: 84 per cent of the coffees drunk are real.

Nancy Astor:
Winston, if I were married to you, I'd put poison in your coffee.
Winston Churchill:
Nancy, if you were my wife, I'd drink it.
from E. Langhorne, *Nancy Astor and her Friends*

THE ROAST

It is the roast that brings the coffee to life. While the right roast will add sparkle to a quality bean it will never rescue a mediocre one. Just as with wine; terroir – the distinctive combination of soil, climate and position – makes a difference that no amount of careful handling can later adjust. On the other hand a bad roast can ruin a good bean: too short and light, and it will taste 'bready', earthy and dull; too long and it will taste thin and burnt.

Each bean has a natural affinity with a level of roast. Kenyan, for instance, favours a medium roast because that does not mask the distinctive fresh taste, or acidity, and it keeps the light fruitiness. Central American beans blossom under a full roast which brings out some of their sweetness.

Green beans (sometimes more white than green) can often improve in storage – Old Brown Java, stored underground, is the classic case. But roasted beans deteriorate quickly, so retailers never roast until strictly necessary.

The principles of roasting, whether several tablespoons in a table-top roaster or 100 kg commercially, are the same. The beans are poured into an enclosed preheated container and are kept moving so that they colour up evenly. Roasting can be done by ear as much as by eye. First there is a random popping as the beans open out slightly, building up to the full pop of a pan of popcorn. (Though popped, good beans must never snap open and grin' at you – only a slight smirk is allowed.) The noise subsides briefly as the beans begin to smoke again and then recommences. By now the beans are ready and the air is filled with the unique aroma of roasting coffee; how much longer they are roasted depends on the depth required and the nerve of the roaster. Leave them too long and the beans will burst into flames; as a commercial roaster reaches 220–230°C the risks are high.

> ❛ Why do they always put mud into coffee on board steamers? Why does the tea generally taste of boiled boots? ❜
>
> W.M. Thackeray,
> *The Kickleburys on the Rhine*

For the trader it's not just a matter of good taste or preventing fires. An average of 20 per cent of the weight of the bean is lost in roasting, a little less for a light roast, a little more for a high roast. It is coffee's version of the angels' share, the proportion of the spirit that evaporates in the cellars of Cognac. That is why cheaper coffees often have a toasty, biscuity flavour. It is the taste of a coffee that has not been properly roasted.

Mild and medium-roast beans are relatively dull coloured. It is only high-roast beans that have such a delicious sheen from the oils driven out through the roast. Some continental roasts for espresso drinking, particularly in Spain, also have a little sugar added to enhance their glamour.

It is possible to roast green beans at home; most mail-order suppliers have a selection. Don't expect to rustle up a roast in your frying pan, though. You need a very hot heat source, preferably a covered pan, and you need to keep the beans moving. You may be able to hunt down a table-top roaster that will do the job. It's a glorious ritual, though it belongs to a leisured time when drinkers could afford to have rituals, and the downside is that it fills the room with smoke and crispy wisps of roasted parchment.

THE GRIND

In an ideal world, say a peaceful weekend morning when the sun is shining, the best way to enjoy a better cup is to grind the beans yourself and then make the coffee immediately. Coffee beans contain essential oils, which are the natural flavour of coffee brought to life by roasting. Beans stay fresher if kept whole and airtight. Grinding releases the oils, allowing the hot water to soak them in the brewing process. It also exposes them to their great enemy – air. That is why coffee from espresso machines that grind and brew in one process tastes so good.

Once upon a time coffee beans were ground with a pestle and mortar or between millstones. No easy job, as the beans would escape from under. Today the best beans are ground using metal 'millstones' with serrated edges. There is now a fairly wide choice of grinders for home use. The best are the ones that still work on the principle of the millstone,

HOW TO STORE COFFEE

Coffee is a fresh product that will fade. The timings given below can be exceeded but the point is that it is better to buy little and often.

Roasted beans will last in an airtight container or the freezer for a month. Ground coffee will be at its best in an airtight container for a fortnight; in a vacuum pack it will last for up to a year.

Don't keep coffee in the fridge because it will be damaged by condensation.

Beans can be stored in the freezer and ground straight from frozen.

Rinse out the jar from time to time and dry it thoroughly – the oils in coffee do go sour.

Don't store coffee next to tea, it'll taint the tea.

Green beans will last for many months in an airtight pack.

whether the hard way, cranked by hand, or electric. Most popular are the small electric choppers that process beans – like cheese or nuts – between two spinning blades. Purists do not like them, because they chop the beans unevenly and the warmth generated releases the essential oils before the coffee is actually brewed. Realists use them because they are quick and easy.

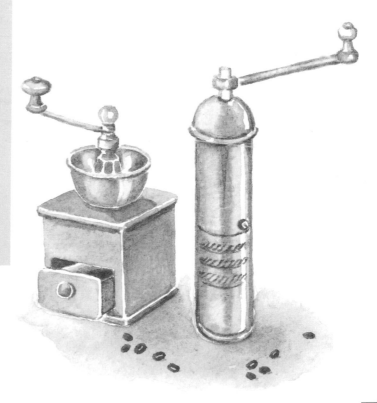

THE METHOD

The great pleasure of making coffee it that it is not in the least complicated. Lke tea, you can be sure of making one cup after another, each consistent, as long as you always keep to the same measurements.

In the early days there was a certain degree of alchemy in the process, typified by the Cona coffee machine that was heated by a little spirit lamp. Today there is a variety of technology to serve our needs but the simplest techniques are often the best. Use a container that can be

FIVE WAYS TO RUIN A CUP OF COFFEE

1 Adding milk that has been overheated – the sugars in the milk caramelize, tainting the coffee. So be sure the milk is only warm, or has been steamed by an espresso machine.
2 Using boiling water – it makes the coffee bitter.
3 Reheating the coffee by bringing it to the boil – only bring it back to the slightest simmer.
4 Mixing up old coffee with new in the same jar.
5 Overmeasuring – you will never make stronger coffee by adding more grains. Buy a stronger roast.

cleaned easily, whether glass, china or stainless steel. Whatever method you use to brew remember certain principles – the freshest grounds, freshly run water, and water that boiled five seconds ago. Unlike tea, coffee shouldn't have boiling water, and, like tea, should never be boiled again. Don't use hot milk unless you can steam heat it in an espresso machine – heated milk risks tainting the coffee with the taste of caramelized sugars. Better to copy the coffee bars – store your cups in a warm place (ideally on top of an espresso machine) to keep the warmth in the coffee.

> ❛ *I have measured out my life with coffee spoons.* ❜
> T.S. Eliot,
> *The Love Song of J. Alfred Prufrock*

The jug

The western version of the Eastern method. Because the grounds are strained off it needs a coarse grind. A favourite of students and impoverished artists. Use a level dessertspoon per person. Add just-boiled water, stir gently and leave to stand for three to four minutes. Strain with a very fine sieve. Because the coffee is strained it has more texture than filtered coffee. If you like your coffee slightly 'chewy', then this is for you. Try medium and French-roast South American and Indonesian. Alternatively, make it the cowboy way, with cold water and ground coffee. Bring to simmering point on the stove; never allow it to boil, or the only thing it will be good for is putting out the fire – John Wayne style.

Coffee sock

A neat variation of the jug method is the small nylon bag that can be put inside a pot or cup. Leave to stand for three minutes and then remove the bag. It's almost as instant as the tea bag. It is messy to wash up but is great for one cup. Use a teaspoon of medium-ground coffee per cup.

Cafetière

Increasingly the most popular choice. It is simple to use and extracts the best of the flavour. Remember this useful formula:

one heaped dessertspoon of beans = one rounded dessertspoon of grounds = 10 g coffee, which is the perfect amount for a three-cup cafetière

three heaped dessertspoons of beans = three rounded dessertspoons of grounds 30 g of coffee = the correct amount for an eight-cup cafetière

Don't be tempted to add that extra half-measure – you'll get thick, 'chewy' coffee.

The major drawback of this method is that users are keen to push the plunger down too early. Leave to stand for four to five minutes, before using the plunger. Another disadvantage is that the coffee gets cold easily. However, this could be seen as a good thing since it encourages drinkers to make a fresh cup every time. Alternatively rinse the pot with a dash of water just before the kettle boils, or buy an insulated jacket for the pots or an insulated cafetière. Always use medium-ground coffee. Cafetières make brilliant medium-strength coffee; try Colombia, Sumatra or Java.

THE STOVE-TOP ESPRESSO The so-called Moka pot, which simply forces the very hot water through *fairly fine* grounds, from the bottom chamber to the top, extracts plenty of flavour. The popular versions are made out of aluminium, but stainless steel is better for a good-tasting cup.

A variation on this is the 'flip' pot, originally from Naples. In this you turn the pot over to filter the coffee when the water is hot. Look for a continental espresso blend, and only ever three-quarters fill the coffee filter using 4–6 g per cup.

ESPRESSO Though invented in the nineteenth century it was Mr Gaggia who created a storm in 1946 with his high-pressure device for forcing water through dark-roast coffee. Home espressos are fun, though you may find that they are never quite as good as a commercial machine. But since the restaurant versions cost several thousand pounds this is perhaps not surprising. The goal of all top *baristas* is to get a thin film of golden froth on their espressos, known as 'crema'. A good guide is 6 g of grounds per person.

TRY OUR
ESPRESSO
CAPPUCCINO
CAFE LATTE
CAFE AU LAIT
CAFE MOCHA
FILTER COFFEE

Espresso Bar

CINN CHOC

PERCOLATOR The centrepiece of 1950s dinner parties, they are now felt to squeeze too much out of the coffee before it even reaches the cup.

COLD COMFORT Remember that coffee does not need these high temperature methods – simply pour on cold water and leave it to stand. It will need several hours to steep but none of the volatile flavours will have been damaged. Or for utter heaven try Tom Stobart's recipe (from *Herbs, Spices and Flavourings*):

For the most exquisite result, if expense is no object, very coarsely ground or cracked freshly roasted coffee is put directly into cream which is at room temperature, a process that extracts only the delicate volatile part of the flavouring. Such cream has the fragrance of freshly roasted coffee without the bitterness.

ICED COFFEE

Using your regular coffee maker, brew the coffee as usual, but making it just a little stronger than usual if you want to add milk. Pour the coffee off the grains into a jug after four or five minutes. Add milk and sugar to the hot coffee at this stage, if required, because they will dissolve far better at this temperature. Chill the coffee, and add crushed ice, which will dilute the stronger brew and make a delicious rich, creamy drink.

WHAT'S WRONG WITH MY COFFEE?

Cafetière coffee isn't hot
Warm the pot by rinsing it first with a dash of boiling water,
just as you would a teapot. Follow the practice of the espresso experts and
serve it in warm cups.

The coffee tastes dull
Use fresh, cold water – let the tap run for a while before you fill the kettle.
Pour the boiled water onto the coffee five seconds after it has boiled – but
don't leave it. Fifteen seconds delay makes all the difference between
delicious and drab coffee.

The coffee tastes bitter
It's a cheap coffee, probably containing Robusta. Always choose pure
Arabica, which is typically bright and spicy. And you may have used too
much coffee – it's a common problem.

I want to reheat coffee without spoiling it
The key is not to boil it. Strain it from the grounds, and you will find it
reheats well in the microwave. Or heat it up in a pan but keep an eye on it
so that it never goes beyond a simmer.

My espresso machine doesn't taste like real espresso
Have you read the instructions carefully? Domestic espresso machines
can work really well but you need to follow the rules. Always 'bleed'
the machine of any stale water before starting by running it through
the steamer valve. This will also get rid of any airlocks.
Now the pipes are clear you can start afresh.
Are you using fresh fine-ground espresso coffee?

My coffee looks grey now I've put milk in it
You have chosen too dark a roast. For a milky coffee you need a full
flavoured variety such as a French-roast Colombia, Celebes or a continental
Santos or Java. That's why after dinner blends always go grey, because
they are black high roasted.

FLAVOURINGS

Cardamom is the classic flavouring for Arab coffee, but try it with an after-dinner blend. Put a few opened pods in the spout of a long-spouted coffeepot for a hint of flavour. Your guests may not approve. Certainly, Lord Byron didn't, describing the banquet with the gorgeous Haidee on her Greek island:

The beverage was various sherbets
Of raisin, orange, and pomegranate juice,
Squeezed through the rind, which makes it best for use.

These were ranged round, each in its crystal ewer,
And fruits, and date-bread loaves closed the repast,
And Mocha's berry, from Arabia pure,
In small fine China cups, came in at last;
Gold cups of filigree made to secure
The hand from burning underneath them placed;
Cloves, cinnamon, and saffron too were boil'd
Up with the coffee, which (I think) they spoil'd.

THREE OTHER USES OF COFFEE BEANS

1 Roast a few beans in a hot pan when you're selling your house and want to create a seductive atmosphere for buyers coming to view.
2 Mix used grounds in with your compost but check with a garden expert first before you spread it on any prized plants.
3 Add 1 tbsp very finely ground espresso beans to 350 g ricotta cheese and 50 g sugar. Beat well until light, then add 2 tbsp rum for a quick dessert.

Lemon divides opinion, just as it does with tea. While a slice of lemon served with an espresso makes an espresso romano, there are many who think lemon kills the flavour of the drink. Chicory also raises the temperature. It was common to use it to extend or substitute for coffee in times of hardship, as during the Second World War. In fact the dried, roasted tap root of chicory was first used at the end of the eighteenth century in Sicily and Holland, However, it was seen as a way of adulterating coffee. Only later did it become an established item. Coffee essence with chicory flavouring and chicory tablets were once popular ingredients with those who had learned to like the substitutes.

Roasted dandelion root is another common substitute, most usually found in health food shops, since it contains no caffeine. Roasted fig also has its fans, and coffee with fig is known as Viennese blend. The cheapest base is malt coffee, made by roasting grain, usually barley, which has already been malted.

Finally, for the adventurous it is important to record that Frederick the Great of Prussia made his coffee with champagne and flavoured it with a spoonful of mustard.

The Republic of Tea, *The Book of Tea and Herbs*, 1993,
   The Cole Group, Santa Rosa, Ca.
Mariage Frères, *L'Art du thé*, Paris, 1994
James Norwood Pratt, *The Tea Lover's Treasury*, 101 Productions, 1982
Alain Stella et al., *The Book of Tea*, Flammarion, n.d.
William H. Ukers, *All About Tea*, New York 1935
Antony Wild, *The East India Company Book of Tea*,
   Harper Collins, 1994

Kenneth Davids, *The Coffee Book*, Whittet Books, 1976
Francesco and Riccardo Illy, *The Book of Coffee*, Abbeville Press, 1989
Claudia Roden, *Coffee*, Faber, 1977
William H. Ukers, *All About Coffee*, second edition, New York, 1935

COFFEE-GROWING AREAS OF THE WORLD